HIGH STORRS SCHOOL
A Journey

Published by **Arc Publishing and Print**
166 Knowle Lane, Bents Green, Sheffield S11 9SJ.
t: 07809 172872 w: www.sheffieldbooks.co.uk

Acknowledgements

Many thanks go to everyone who has supplied photographs and information for this book. We didn't have room for it all so apologies if your contribution isn't here. Particular thanks go to High Storrs School staff who made this book a reality: Sandra Careless, Tony Dobson, Ian Gage, Abi Merritt and Claire Pender.

In particular the support of Hazel and Sydney Hoffman is much appreciated. Former pupils, Sydney then taught at the school from 1953 to 1981. In 1983 he compiled a history of the school to mark the 50th anniversary. This unpublished work was of huge assistance in compiling the early part of this book.

The book would not have been possible without the efforts of Mary Hickes and Heather Uhlar of the High Storrs Centralians Association who spent many hours locating photographs and documents from their extensive archive.

Thanks go to the staff at the Local Studies Department of Sheffield Central Library, and Sheffield Newspapers Limited for permission to use the photographs from their collection on pages 24 and 25.

Thanks to Vinci Construction UK for their sponsorship in support of this book.

Text copyright 2011 © High Storrs School

The rights of High Storrs School and its work has been asserted by them in accordance with the Copyright, Design Patent Act 1988

September 2011

ISBN: 978-1-906722-20-3

Published by Arc Publishing and Print
166 Knowle Lane
Sheffield
S11 9SJ

Telephone 07809 172872

Foreword

What an excellent idea to ask ex-students of this terrific school and those who have an interest in the 130 year history of High Storrs, to contribute to bringing alive the experiences, the ups and downs and the contribution made to both the life chances of students and the well being of Sheffield, through the last century.

Those of us long enough in the tooth to recall the headquarters of Sheffield's education service in their Leopold Street offices, will also be aware of the location of High Storrs as the then Central School.

Some of us remember the excellent Chair of Governors of High Storrs, Sandra Tomlinson, who took on the chair of the National Governors Association and worked closely with me, both when I took on the role of Shadow Education Secretary and then before her tragic early death, as the Education and Employment Secretary in the first term of the Blair Government.

High Storrs has been a pioneer, including in the delivery of high quality comprehensive education over the last forty years, maintaining the highest standards and commitment to the wider Sheffield community.

I know that High Storrs will go from strength to strength and will continue to collaborate with schools across the city to build on the simple truth; schools that work together and that reach out to family and community produce the highest possible standards and the most active and valued citizens.

This publication is a way of saying thank you to past staff, governors and friends of the school and of course to recognise the achievements of proud and valued students over the last hundred years.

David Blunkett MP

Introduction

Whenever ex-colleagues, old school friends from High Storrs and Centralians gather the conversation soon turns to the inevitable memories of life at High Storrs School. This is also true for any school in the country. For the pre-war generation there will be stories of forbidden contact with school friends of the opposite sex, arranging meetings after school far enough away from the disapproving eyes of the school staff. They will recall the school moving from Leopold Street to High Storrs Road and the challenges this presented to pupils trying to get to school. In the post-war years there will be recollections of flying blackboard rubbers and chalk, terrifying disciplinarians and teachers who shaped lives and inspired careers. In the seventies the memories will recall the change to the comprehensive system and the academic and sporting prowess of individuals and teams. In the new century discussion will turn to school trips, artistic performances, the condition of the buildings, the refurbishment and the fantastic new facilities now available for pupils at the school.

This book unites all those memories and will provoke even more about life at High Storrs School. 'Those were the Days' 'Can you remember the time when...?' 'What was the name of that teacher who taught...?'

Ian Gage

High Storrs School has come through a major building programme and creditably it has continued to improve. This is a testament to staff, parents and students. We now have a magnificent building which matches the rich and varied talent of our students whilst reflecting the important history of the school. A 1930s building has been made fit for the 21st century and we can feel proud to be a part of its future.

I hope you enjoy this photographic journey through some of our history.

Ian Gage (Headteacher)

Index

Chapter 1

THE CENTRAL SECONDARY SCHOOL

The history of High Storrs School can be traced back to the Elementary Education Act of 1870. Before that date education was not compulsory and education was provided by private fee paying or church-funded schools. Many children received no education at all. Sheffield factories employed children as young as six for long hours and in dirty and dangerous conditions. Many people campaigned for better treatment and education of children, but another factor encouraged the introduction of compulsory education. As Britain expanded its trade and influence as an imperial power its manufactured goods were in demand across the globe. Sheffield was a world leader in the production of both cutlery and steel. A shift from manual work in small workshops to machine production in large factories required a more educated workforce to operate complex machinery but also to support production and trade through account keeping, advertising and the keeping of production records.

The 1870 Act introduced compulsory education for children up to the age of ten, and local School Boards were established by the government to manage this process. In November 1870 the Sheffield School Board was created and the first school to be built in England under the Act was Newhall School at Attercliffe in 1873. Fourteen further Sheffield Board Schools were built over the next few years. At this time the area between Orchard Lane, West Street, Orchard Street and Balm Green was a warren of slums. The site was bought by the Sheffield School Board and cleared to build schools and offices for themselves. The steel magnate Mark Firth planned to create a University College and the Board sold him part of the site at the corner of West Street. The new building – Firth College - was opened by Queen Victoria's son Prince Leopold in 1879 and the street named in his honour.

In 1880 the Central Schools on Leopold Street were opened by the 6th Earl Spencer (great-grandfather of the late Diana, Princess of Wales). These included Infant and Junior Schools but also the Sheffield Central Higher Grade School, a secondary school created chiefly to provide entrants to Firth College. The Sheffield School Board had no legal authority or mandate to provide secondary education, but in doing so they created what was essentially the first state secondary school of its type in the country, where entry was based on merit rather than wealth or class. Boys and girls were admitted by examination from all the Board's elementary (primary) schools. Other School Boards followed Sheffield's lead but it was many years before such secondary schools were officially recognised in law.

The original school building on Orchard Lane.

Throughout the latter years of the 19th Century the Leopold Street site was expanded to provide more school places and a teacher training centre was added to provide staff for the growing school system in Sheffield. In 1900 the government realised the school's provision of education to the age of 18 was illegal, and all those over 15 years of age had to leave. This situation was remedied by the 1902 Education Act, and the new Sheffield Education Committee took over the functions of the Sheffield School Board. This Committee had the authority to provide secondary education and in 1904 it was officially recognised as a secondary school.

The Girls' Grammer School (formerly Firth College) pictured in 1919.

In 1897 Firth College and the nearby Sheffield Technical College had merged with the Sheffield Medical School to form the University College of Sheffield. In 1905 this received its Royal Charter and became the University of Sheffield moving to new buildings on Western Bank. The Central School split into a girl's school which occupied the former Firth College, with the boys remaining in the original buildings.

The first girl's sixth form in 1907.

The school at this time had no playing fields and physical education was conducted in the asphalted yard of the school. Ball games led to windows of the school being regularly broken, and football or cricket matches could only be played as 'away' fixtures or occasionally in places such as Endcliffe Park. Now that the school was formally recognised as a secondary school the Education Committee had a duty to ensure it had adequate facilities, including playing fields.

In 1899 the council had acquired three fields totalling 36 acres at High Storrs opposite "Mr Roberts' Marsh Farm" on High Lane (now called Ringinglow Road). At that time Sheffield was much smaller than now, with little housing west of Banner Cross apart from farm workers' cottages and a few grand houses set in their own grounds. The land at High Storrs was originally purchased to provide council housing, but local opposition and the distance from industry rendered it unsuitable for this purpose. The land was transferred to the Education Committee and in 1904 given to the school as playing fields. The school at this time was also renamed the Central Secondary School. Another development in 1904 was school meals at a price of "5d (2p) for scholars and 6d (2$^{1}/_{2}$p) for staff".

The field nearest what is now Ringinglow Road was allocated to the boys' school, the middle one to the teacher training college, and the furthest to the girls' school. Each form would visit on one afternoon each week or fortnight, travelling by tram to Ecclesall Terminus and then following field paths on the slopes now occupied by the houses of Knowle Lane and Hoober Avenue. The initial activity however was not play but work. Much toil by pupils and staff turned rough land into playing fields and by 1906 the school was able to enjoy the first of many annual sports days. Another annual event was the Girls v Boys Cricket match. This was usually a closely fought fixture aided by the fact that the boys had to bat, bowl and field left-handed!

At the Sports Day of 9 July 1914 a group of boys and teachers set up a radio installation on the field and were able to receive radio messages broadcast from the Eiffel Tower in Paris. By 28 July the Great War was underway and the 1915 school magazine records "The school wireless equipment was sealed up by the government in the early days of the war. Now the essential parts have been collected and taken away. Let us hope it may soon be returned for then the war will be over". Unfortunately those hopes were in vain. By 1918 what we now know as the First

Girls' Sports Day around 1910 at High Storrs.

World War had left over 16 million people dead and many more seriously injured.

Girls' Three-legged race around 1910.

942 old boys of the school fought in the war, with 161 losing their lives including 2nd Lieutenant Robert Vine of the Cambridgeshire Regiment. His story is better known than most as his family gave records and photographs to the school after the war, but it is typical of the millions of such men, many of them just teenagers, whose lives were cut short by war.

Robert Saxelby Vine was born in Attercliffe in 1891, the only son of George Robert Vine. George Vine was a teacher at the Central School, before becoming the head of Hunter's Bar School and latterly Huntsman's Gardens School in Attercliffe. By 1898 the family were living at 10 Ranby Road near to Endcliffe Park. Robert attended the Central Secondary School, and was a founder member of the school's Shakespeare Society. In 1906 aged 14 he played Fluellen in Henry V, a fictional Captain of the English King's army fighting in France during the Hundred Year's War. No photograph of this production exists, but from early in the 20th century until the outbreak of the Second World War the boy's school performed one of Shakespeare's plays each year. In the finest tradition of Elizabethan theatre all the cast were male with boys enthusiastically donning dresses, makeup and wigs to play the female parts.

Robert Vine (second from right) with school friends in 1906.

Robert Vine with his fiancée Elsie Palmer on holiday in Wales - Summer 1914.

After school Robert gained a place at Sheffield University where he graduated in 1913, and in 1914 gained an MA there. Later that year he took up a post as a teacher at March Grammar School in Cambridgeshire, and also married one Elsie Palmer. Prospects of a comfortable family life in rural England were soon overturned by events elsewhere in Europe. Just nine years after portraying an English army officer Robert volunteered to take on that role again, this time swapping the innocent camaraderie of a school production for the horrors of war. He enlisted with his local Cambridgeshire Regiment as part of 1/1st Battalion which landed at Le Havre in France on 15 February 1915. From there they were deployed to the trenches of northern France and Belgium. The most notable action for the battalion was the capture of the Schwaben Redoubt in October 1916 during the Battle of the Somme. This strong German fortress dominated the area around the village of Thiepval and the Ancre River, a tributary of the Somme. Successive attacks by allied forces had failed to capture it. It was finally gained on 15 October by the 1/1st Battalion together with the 4/5th Black Watch after hours of bitter fighting and severe losses.

The battle was the subject of a special commendation by Field Marshall Haig, Commander-in-Chief of the British Expeditionary Force, who referred to it as 'one of the finest feats of arms in the history of the British Army'. This achievement cost the battalion 213 men killed or badly wounded. One of those killed was Robert Vine who died on 14 October 1916 at the height of the battle. He was just 24 years of age. Those at school helped the war effort in their own way. Parts of the sports field at High Storrs were tended by pupils as vegetable allotments, and by 1918 the school was growing all its own potatoes for school dinners.

Edna Blackwell

Edna Blackwell was one of the first girls to go on to Sheffield University in 1918. In 1922 she was elected President of the Student's Union.

School production of Antony and Cleopatra in 1920.
Alfred Lidster as Antony, J. Sydney Ash as Cleopatra.

The Gentlewomen
in 'The Taming of
the Shrew' in 1921.
All played by boys.

School production
of 'The Taming of
the Shrew' in 1921.
Algernon R. Garner
as a Gentlewoman.

Traditional May Day celebrations date back to pagan times marking the end of winter and the start of spring. These traditions were adopted by Christians throughout Europe and interwoven with Easter celebrations. During the 17th Century Puritanical opinion suppressed the tradition because of its crude pagan origins and the practice disappeared. In the latter part of the 19th Century John Ruskin (then Slade Professor of Art at Oxford University) revived the tradition as a celebration of an earlier time before the industrial revolution when people lived simple lives in what he regarded as rural idylls.

The Central School adopted the tradition in 1900, with one girl being chosen each year by her peers, and named after a flower. The ceremonies took place in the Albert Hall in nearby Barker's Pool (now demolished) and then in the Victoria Hall until the building of the City Hall in the 1930s when the ceremony moved there. Since any girl in the Lower Sixth could be chosen the dress was made to fit the largest girl, and then once the decision was made the dress was quickly adapted to fit on the day! The dresses were elaborate works of art, hand-made and embroidered by staff and pupils. The chosen girl then took up the duties of Head Girl for the following school year.

The tradition continued until 1939 and the start of the Second World War. The lavish ceremonies were no longer appropriate, and in any event the rationing of dress material meant that the creation of a dress for a single ceremony was impossible.

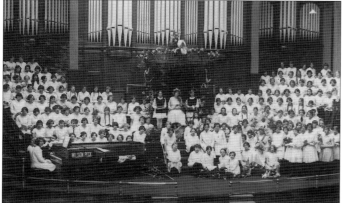

May Day Celebrations of 1930 in the Victoria Hall.

Edith Willey was chosen as the May Queen of 1913 – the second Apple Blossom of the school's tradition. Born in 1895 to George Willey, a warehouse manager and his wife Ellen, she was one of five children. In 1900 tragedy struck the family when George died leaving Ellen to bring up five children in the days before widow's pensions or other state support. In such circumstances families were often broken up, with younger children sent to orphanages or adopted by relatives or childless couples, and older siblings working. Ellen would have none of this and supported her family by opening a grocery shop which she ran with the help of her eldest daughter Ethel. Edith attended St Stephen's Church of England School near their shop in the Netherthorpe area of Sheffield. At the age of ten she won entrance to the Central Secondary School where she excelled at all subjects, and by 1914 she had secured a place at Somerville College, Oxford. Edith was one of the first women to study at either Oxford or Cambridge.

Three years of May Queens - Edith Willey Apple Blossom II 1913, Kathleen Hydes Primrose II 1912, Edith Hitchins Daisy II 1911.

Although awarded a scholarship this covered barely half the tuition fees and she was only able to go to university with the support of her older brother (also George) who was working as a metallurgist in Sheffield.

She studied history from 1914 until 1917 when she was awarded 2nd class honours, but prior to 1920 women were not allowed to matriculate and therefore she was not awarded a degree or recognised as a member of the university! Despite attending lectures and passing exams alongside her fellow male students she was not awarded her BA degree until December 1920. Edith had an illustrious career as a history teacher in Newcastle, Bristol and Leeds before securing a position as Headmistress of Clapham County School in London where she worked for 18 years until her retirement in 1956. She died in West Harnham near Salisbury in 1970 having never married.

Although a pioneer in her own way Edith's success was matched by many of her fellow pupils at the Central Secondary School. By 1933 a total of 52 scholarships had been won for Oxford and Cambridge and over 300 pupils had gone on to other universities, particularly Sheffield and London.

A needlework class in 1919

A boys' chemistry lesson in 1920.

1922 BOYS' SCHOOL ORCHESTRA
February 24th.

Boys' Orchestra 1922.

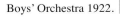

Christine Thompson - Primrose IV in 1939.
The last May Queen.

Chapter 2

HIGH STORRS AND WORLD WAR 2

The Central School had served its original purpose well, but as more secondary schools were built across Sheffield the convenient location was outweighed by the disadvantages of the now cramped site and lack of open space. In 1931 the Education Committee decided a new school was needed and the playing fields at High Storrs were the obvious site. The new school, in what is now known as Art Deco style, was designed by the City Architect WG Davies FRIBA. A Sheffield building company, WG Robson Limited of Bamforth Street was awarded the contract, and by 1933 the school was complete at a cost of £95,053. This was considered excellent value. The building work disrupted the use of the site as playing fields and at least two football pitches were lost. One of these, close to Ringinglow Road, was regarded as the "best amateur pitch in Sheffield". The construction was of a high standard using the best materials and the facilities were the best of their day. The building was designed as two schools, with the south wing reserved for boys and the north being the girls' school. The shared assembly hall was placed centrally, flanked by a dining room for each school but served by a single kitchen. The quadrangles were to be areas of 'quiet tranquillity' with their lawns and stone-flagged paths. Open corridors on both sides overlooked two sides of the quadrangles.

The boys' quadrangle.

The girls' quadrangle.

A typical classroom in the new school.

The front facade of the school in 1933. The now demolished caretaker's house can be seen at the far end.

The Chemistry Laboratory.

The Domestic Science Room.

One of the two Dining Halls.

The Boys' Gymnasium.

The open balconies and cloisters facing the quadrangles may have been pleasant in June, but by winter the harsh weather of an exposed site 750 feet above sea level filled them with snow, sleet and rain on a regular basis. In 1939 £900 was spent enclosing them creating the corridors of today's building.

Trainee PE teachers from Leopold Street continued to use the sports facilities at High Storrs after the new school opened.

The opening ceremony on Wednesday 28 June 1933 was performed by The Lord Mayor of London Sir Percy W Greenaway. A coach and horses brought him from the railway station but the steep gradient of Ringinglow Road was too much for the horses, and taxis had to be summoned to complete the journey. Oak trees were planted by the Lord Mayor in the school grounds.

The school retained its original name and it was not until 1940 that logic prevailed and it was renamed High Storrs Grammar School.

The Lord Mayor of London's procession along Ecclesall Road.

The Lord Mayor and Lady Mayoress of London are greeted by pupils

1938 brought the Munich Crisis and Europe slipped towards war. Soldiers were stationed on the school field and anti-aircraft guns were set up. With the advent of World War 2 in September 1939 much of the centre of the field was taken up by a mysterious 'Bomb-Bouncer' (in reality a radar aerial).

Miss Battensby, the Headmistress of the Girls' Grammar School during the war later recorded her memories:

"First came "Home Service". It was not considered safe to have large numbers at school until the underground shelters were built, so we used over one hundred meeting places all over the city (many in private houses) where not more than twenty girls at a time were taught. The staff - in bus or on bicycle or sturdy legs - became itinerant teachers. Many were the tales they had to tell when we met to compare experiences at the end of each week, and many were the problems. The carting and distribution of books was a nightmare. Practical subjects suffered most. Physical training was a joke but we survived. We learnt a lot about the city and about teaching. We kept it up for several months until the underground shelters were ready. Then we shared the building with Abbeydale [School] and the ARP and the games field with anti-aircraft gunners".

Air raid shelters were dug close to the school building, and parts of the field were again used for vegetable production. Senior pupils slept in the building each night on fire-watching duty.

Thursday 12 December 1940 brought the horror of the warfare into the heart of Sheffield. During that night and again on the night of the 15th, the German Luftwaffe dropped thousands of bombs across Sheffield, destroying thousands of homes and factories. The Sheffield Blitz killed 660 people with many more injured and thousands made homeless. High Storrs had escaped the worst of this. On the morning of Friday 13 December staff came to school as normal. Schools and other public buildings still intact were designated as rest centres for the injured and homeless, and between 400 and 500 people were brought to High Storrs School. For many it was their home for weeks, and the school was closed to pupils until the middle of January 1941. Teachers and older pupils cared for the evacuees, clearing classrooms to provide sleeping spaces. Some staff went around all local households begging tins of food, and it was from this generosity that the evacuees were fed for the first two or three days until the authorities were able to organise deliveries of food.

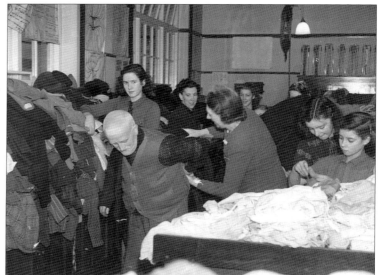

Many evacuees arrived at High Storrs with no personal belongings and were provided with clothes donated by more fortunate residents.

Children at the rest centre were provided with toys and books donated by local residents.

A soldier helps distribute food in the High Storrs rest centre.

Betty McPherson (née Thorold) a pupil between 1935 and 1942 remembered those days:

"On the night of the blitz I was doing my geography homework and listening to ITMA. Those of us who lived near went up to school the next day to find that the building had become a rest centre and was full of pathetic, homeless people. We collected and made clothes, tried to deter mothers from feeding babies on evaporated milk clearly marked 'unfit for babies'; there was a field kitchen in the quad and chaos everywhere. We wondered about friends who lived on the other side of the city, but when we returned to school, there they all were, even though one of them had been at the Empire Theatre when it all happened. Fortunately, very few High Storrs girls were killed that night."

Like many city centre buildings the Empire Theatre in Charles Street had suffered a direct hit from a large bomb which killed and injured many people, including musicians on the stage.

In early 1941 JF Leaper was the first Old Boy of the school to be killed in action and by the end of the war a total of 67 former pupils had lost their lives.

Empire Theatre 1933.

As the war ended school life slowly returned to normal. The division of the school into Boys' and Girls' Schools is remembered:

"The boys' Grammar School was housed in the left side of the building and we were on the right. Only the hall and dining rooms were communal but we were never in them at the same time. There were not a lot of chances to meet. Boys started and finished at different times and our dinner hour overlapped by around ten minutes. The boys were usually returning from 'The Roughs' at dinnertime just as we were going there and after school the girls would hang around for the boys to come out. When we had Ancient Greek style dancing in the hall, the grills under the stage would be full of boys' faces peering out at us and we never knew how they managed to be under the stage in class time."

Margaret Sanderson 1950 to 1955

The Entrance Hall Oval in the 1950s.

A Science class
in the 1950s.

A woodwork class in the 1950s.

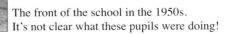

The front of the school in the 1950s.
It's not clear what these pupils were doing!

Break time in the 1950s.

Alan Stephenson came to High Storrs Grammar School in 1955, leaving to train as a Biology teacher and securing his first job at his old school in 1966.

"I arrived at High Storrs Grammar School for Boys in 1955 from Prince Edward County Junior School with about 6 or 7 other boys and I did not like the place at all. Looking back, the school was trying to imitate the traditional public school. Rigid school uniform, blazers with badges, blue /green quarter caps, ties, prefects with green braid and tassels on caps, lording over the rest of the school and rules which must be obeyed.

The annual school cross country run was a highlight for me, but not for many others. We all had to run, no excuses, (though there were always some) Juniors, Intermediates and Seniors were run separately. I would probably have been quite miserable had it not been for these competitions. I had many other teachers for whom I had the greatest respect, some were inspirational, making me realise that I would enjoy teaching. So it was, in 1966 I became assistant Biology teacher to my old friend and colleague Ken Sale. I was the first appointment made by the new Headmaster, the late Tim Mardell and I never left until retirement in 2004. I guess I was just born lucky."

Alan Stephenson 1955 to 1962, 1966 to 2004 (as staff)

Alan Stephenson in 1957.

1970s Sports Day. Alan Stephenson
as timekeeper (centre left in glasses)

Ollie Smith (left) as one
of the Young Princes
in Richard III 1956.

Ollie Smith also attended the school as a pupil and then returned to teach English, Drama and Theatre Studies there until his retirement. Both Alan and Ollie were Heads of House with the houses taking their names.

HIGH STORRS SCHOOL

"After passing the 11-plus, I started at High Storrs in September 1956 and stayed until I had taken my A levels. I had many good times there, especially on the football and cricket pitches, and some not so good, such as the occasions when I was caned, sometimes fairly and sometimes without justification. However, my overriding memory is of a very traditional grammar school with firmly established structures. When I left in 1963, it never entered my mind that I would ever return. After graduating and completing my PGCE year in 1967, I needed a short term job so when the incumbent Head, Tim Mardell, offered me a post in the English Department, I accepted it with a few qualms. I told myself it would only be for a year and the thought that I would spend the rest of my working life in my old school horrified me. But my wife started her career in Sheffield and I was fortunate enough to be promoted internally quite quickly so that by 1974 I was Head of the 17-strong and highly successful English Department.

In 1981 I became Head of one of the four Houses, then called Catliffe, Stephenson, Smith and Warner. I had always been enthusiastic about the House system; indeed, I had been very proud to be House Captain of Goths in my final year as a pupil but it initially felt strange to have a House named after me. These years were amongst the most challenging and rewarding of my career.

I was frequently humbled by the trust placed in me by both students and parents and filled with admiration at the way in which people bravely faced up to educational, social, medical, financial and personal problems. Above all, I did my best to guide the young people in Smith House through the confusing process of growing up and to help them make the most of their educational opportunities.

I wouldn't recommend this career path to anyone else, but in retrospect, I wouldn't change any of it. I still cannot think any other career which could have given me anything like the job satisfaction I gained. For that, I have to thank many colleagues and thousands of wonderful High Storrs students."

Ollie Smith, around 1990.

Ollie Smith 1956 to 1963, 1967 to 2004 (as staff)

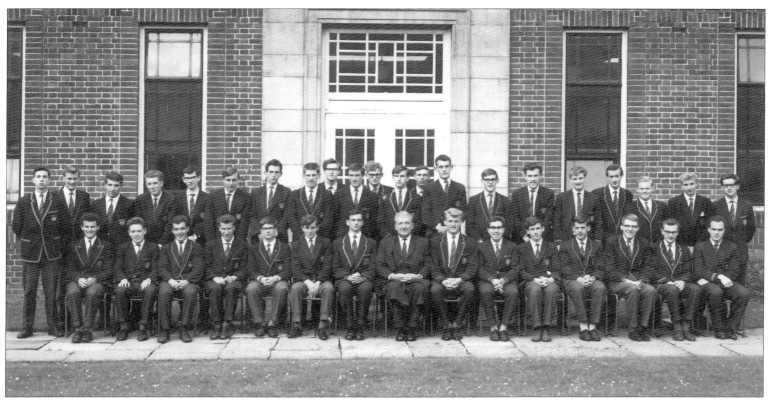

George Mack with prefects in 1963. Ollie Smith is bottom left.

The journalist, writer and broadcaster Paul Heiney recalls his time at High Storrs.

"I consider that winning a place at High Storrs was one of the great turning points in my life. I was the first person in our wider family to go to a grammar school. Looking back, there was much that was badly taught (English) and much that was inspiring (Chemistry taught by Alf Ridler). But the strangest thing about the place was the girls' school next door which was joined to the boys' school in every way except socially. It was an offence to socialise with the girls at the bus stop - you could get detention for that! Incidentally, in case there is any confusion, I changed my name when I started to broadcast and so you will find no reference to Paul Heiney in the school records. It was Paul Wisniewski in those days, and I was a very fat boy!"

Paul Wisniewski/Heiney 1961 to 1967

Paul Heiney.

35

New dining room 1963.

The old library in 1963.

Form 5F in 1961.

Domestic Science room 1963.

New art room in 1963.

Ray Everitt came to High Storrs in 1975 to teach Classics and Latin

"I joined High Storrs as a bright young probationer in 1975, complete with hair, leather jacket and purple suede boots. My plan was to do a couple of years and then move on. A few months later and I realised that High Storrs was one of the few state schools that offered Classics, and I could not see myself as a teacher in the independent sector.

I remember with fondness the many valued pupils and teachers I came to know, especially those associated with Classics. It has always been a popular but niche subject, and the efforts of Colin Smith, Kath Bampton and John Nicholls helped to keep it as a vibrant and viable subject in the curriculum. More recently Rosemary Hulse and Gina Johnson in particular have kept the flag flying. "Floreat Latina!" We were also lucky to have Headteachers like Cheryle Berry, and now Ian Gage, who have been most supportive.

A boy in my first ever A level class eventually became godfather to my daughter Jessica; others have kept in touch and last year I was moved to receive an excellent book of Classical myths from a pupil who wrote on the flyleaf. "Thanks for teaching me Classics in 1982. Sorry I was awful!"

They are just two examples of the thousands of wonderful, caring, mature and thoughtful pupils that High Storrs has produced over the years. Long may it continue. As we see the brilliant new and refurbished areas we can rest assured that the school will go from strength to strength. I had a brilliant time for 36 years and I owe the school a debt which cannot ever be paid."

Ray is pictured in Sri Lanka in 2009 visiting a school rebuilt with funds raised by High Storrs School.

Victoria Shortland attended the school as a pupil and now teaches there.
She particularly recalls the change from grammar to comprehensive school.

*"It was a very bright and sunny morning on
6th September 1969. I checked my makeup in my dad's
driving mirror and waited until he had driven off before
rolling my school skirt at the waistband to make it as
short as I dared. This was the day I had waited for.
The double doors to the boys' school were unlocked and
opened, we were 'to be mixed with the boys'. We had
gone 'Comprehensive'.*

*We had all lessons with the boys except the 'non
academic'. The girls were not allowed to learn woodwork,
the boys not domestic science. Funnily enough the domestic science teacher was called Mrs Kitchen."*

Victoria Shortland (née Campbell)

Tim Mardell became Head of
the Boys' School in 1966 and
in 1969 became Head of the
merged school as a
comprehensive.

Mike Brady was Head of PE at High Storrs from 1967 to 1982 and then Head of Careers Guidance and Work Experience until his retirement in 1994.

"High Storrs has always been a highly successful school. Historically it has always had a caring, multi-talented, diverse community, from all parts of Sheffield. The plays, musicals, concerts for orchestra, wind band, choirs, and jazz bands have produced many outstanding successes with students graduating to the amateur and professional ranks, in music, drama and dance. Joe Cocker played in the school library in 1968 and was booked, together with the Ebbonites, by me for the princely sum of £25. What a steal! In past years the school had

an annual summer fete. We attracted many notable celebrities including Olivia Newton-John, an aerial display with parachutists, bound for another fête, but landing at High Storrs instead, what a bonus! Fortunately Health & Safety were not so evident then. The biggest success by far has been the ability of the whole High Storrs community to imbue and develop personal confidence in the majority of its students. That is by far the most precious gift that anyone can possess and the students were given that option in abundance.
Past students please note that Black Jack and Back Slap were not real; they were a part of a mythical legend that circulates to this day."

Sixth Formers in 1982.

Kate Stow taught English at High Storrs from 1972 until 2007 and for many years was the Head of Post-16 Education.

"I always maintained that Head of Sixth Form was the best job in the school. It certainly wasn't because it was easy, far from it. The beginning of the school year was always chaotic, firstly because we were still trying to finalise university places for the previous year's Y13s, secondly the new Y12s were being admitted, there were always problems with their timetables, sometimes daily changes to be accommodated and often latecomers to fit in. At the same time we needed to make an early start on UCAS forms for new Y13s particularly for those applying for Oxford or Cambridge, Medicine, Dentistry or Veterinary Science. The summer holidays only ever lasted three weeks as we prepared for results and then spent time in school helping with clearing.

From 1993 the prom was held at Baldwin's Omega and was the highlight of the year. I enjoyed the joke presentations, things like 'Best Excuse for Not Completing Coursework', 'Teacher's Pet', 'Boffin' or Most Eligible Bachelor'. Couples also got awards and many of the recipients are still couples today."

Kate Stow

High Storrs Prom 2007.

Peter Kennett taught Geology from 1971 until his retirement in 1999. Pictured are a group of Geology students on a field trip to Wenlock Edge in 1972.

Robin Towle was Deputy Head between 1977 and 2000 and worked with Headteachers Tim Mardell, Cheryle Berry and Liz Talmadge.

"Tim Mardell was one of the first generation of comprehensive heads, who believed in a grammar school education for all. There was school uniform, corporal punishment, a 'remedial' department of one person, and a very large academic 6th Form.

For Tim's first Speech Day he had invited Jimmy Reid, the communist convener of the Govan shipyard. This provoked an outcry from the Ecclesall parents, so the following year he had Edward Heath. Staff who were there said these two were the best speakers they had heard but by 1977 there was a succession of academics and sports stars that made the disciplinary job of the form tutors down on the floor of the Hall impossible. They were impressive occasions for those parents in the upper tiers who were mostly unaware of the frantic attempts to control the bored teenagers in the stalls.

The end came when Tim in 1979 invited the Education Secretary for the following year. He was hoping to get Shirley Williams but Labour unexpectedly lost the election and we got Mark Carlisle, Mrs Thatcher's appointee. Special Branch were in touch with the school a couple of weeks before the event, surprising senior staff by their knowledge of one of our pupils who was the leader of the newly formed union of school students, and the City Hall was searched from top to bottom on the day. At Speech Day, the Chair of Governors, Dr Julian Kinderlerer, attacked Carlisle in his speech for his visit earlier in the day to 'the most unrepresentative school in the city', Birkdale; parents and pupils heckled Carlisle's speech; some parents unfurled 'Tory Out' banners; the smell of stink bombs arose from the corridors and a deputy head caused unnecessary alarm to the special guests afterwards by dropping a couple of confiscated cap bombs outside their meeting room. Tim sat with his morale boosting smile throughout the proceedings but we never had another Speech Day.

Tim was Head during the dreadful teacher disputes of the 1980s but he was never flustered, never lost his temper (though sometimes claiming to be 'feeling irritable'), was very quick in debate and could out talk the most vociferous opponent. He died in 2001.

Cheryl Berry was very different. She held an interview with every member of staff in her first few weeks, ran an open door policy for staff, was always approachable, and was, above all, very positive about the school, its pupils and its staff, and had almost the emotional response towards the school of a mother towards her family.

Cheryle also tried to improve the deteriorating environment of the school on a very limited budget. Windows were jammed open or fast shut so that you boiled in summer and froze in winter. The boilers broke down at least once a year, often seeming to choose the coldest day of the year. Parts of the school leaked every time there was heavy rain. It is remarkable that teachers and pupils still produced the excellent results they did.

Sixth Formers decorating the common room in 1991.

Some of the staff from around 1990.

Cheryle set about these problems with her usual determination. Parents and teachers were drafted in on Saturdays for painting and cleaning sessions.

And then there was Ofsted. Cheryle rang up the Deputy Heads on Boxing Day (or was it Christmas Day?) to tell us she had been to school and discovered a letter announcing the first Ofsted visit. (Deputies always took their phones off the hook at Christmas for the rest of her headship.) This Ofsted was a soft affair, mainly consisting of local authority personnel who knew the school. When this deputy head patrolled 'smokers' corners' to make sure offenders were moved along before the inspectors found them, one inspector was discovered sharing his ciggies with the kids.

Head Teacher Cheryle Berry celebrates a successful first Ofsted Inspection in 1994.

HIGH STORRS SCHOOL

How different from our second Ofsted after Cheryle had left and Liz Talmadge had arrived. The Lead Inspector announced herself to the full staff meeting as 'a Rottweiler' and it was only Liz's persistence and arguments that prevented us from receiving the damning comment of a 'cruising school'. If we had been cruising it had certainly felt like full speed ahead.

Liz knew that she had a lot of work to do. Whereas Cheryle had met each member of staff individually, Liz watched every one of us teach. We were being brought into the 21st century."

Robin Towle

Deputy Heads in 2000. Left to right, Mervyn Bell, Robin Towle, Sarah Rowlands.

Claire Pender came to High Storrs in 1992 as a student teacher and was appointed as an English/Drama teacher in 1993. At that time the Head of Drama was Rob Tomlinson, an inspirational teacher who had continued to build on the tradition of high quality Drama productions at the school.

When Rob left Claire took on the role of Head of Drama and over the years has progressed to Assistant Head Teacher with responsibility for Teaching and Learning.

"In 2002 High Storrs was designated as a specialist school in Performing Arts based on the strength of Drama and Music. At this time we introduced Dance as a discrete subject under the leadership of Moyra Lee who introduced Dance to the curriculum via street dance which proved to be a massive hit, especially with boys.

Dance, Drama and Music have continued to go from strength to strength. All KS3 pupils have lessons in Performing Arts and we offer varied and popular courses at GCSE and A level. High Storrs continues to offer many extra-curricular opportunities to pupils in the form of Dance and Drama clubs, bands and orchestras.

We regularly perform our annual school productions as part of Sheffield Children's Festival and have performed at the Crucible Theatre, Studio Theatre and the City Hall Oval and Memorial Halls over the past few years. Such amazing memories! In 2007 we were designated a second specialism in Maths and Computing and were also delighted to receive the Artsmark Gold award in 2008 in recognition of the high profile of the arts in school.

It's such a pleasure to work at High Storrs. We have a very committed and loyal staff and a wonderful student body, whose talents never fail to amaze us. I have many happy memories of Drama and Theatre Studies classes and feel privileged to have shared groups with inspirational teachers such as Ollie Smith, Lindsey Broughton and Thom Disney."

Claire Pender

'West Side Story' 2005.

Elliot Goodhill as Billy Elliot
at the Crucible Theatre 2011.

49

As a child in the 1970s Geoffrey Crossland was inspired by TV stars Lena Zavaroni and Bonnie Langford. Unfortunately his enthusiasm for singing and dancing wasn't shared by his teachers, one of whom suggested he ought to be thinking about a 'proper job'. Ignoring this advice he left High Storrs for the Italia Conti School in London at the age of 15 and a year later was dancing in 'Pennies from Heaven' in the West End with Tommy Steele. He has worked as a dancer and singer ever since.

Geoffrey Crossland with Bonnie Langford in 'Me and My Girl'.

Tom Ellis left High Storrs to attend The Royal Scottish Academy of Music and Drama. Since graduating in 2000 he has had a highly successful career on television and the stage as well as in film. His numerous television credits include Miranda, Doctor Who and EastEnders. He appeared in the films Vera Drake and Buffalo Soldiers, and has worked in theatres across the country.

"I can't stress how grateful I am to have been a pupil at High Storrs. I was always encouraged to pursue the career I wanted to and the teachers I had helped me realise that. I am especially grateful to Claire Pender who believed in me from the start and always encouraged and supported my dreams. It's a great school with an exceptional Drama Department and looking back I realise how blessed I am to have been there."

Tom Ellis

Tom Ellis as Oberon and Caitlin Smith as Titania in the 1997 Crucible Theatre production of 'A Midsummer Night's Dream'.

51

Chapter 4

HIGH STORRS IN THE 21ST CENTURY

By the start of the 21st Century the fabric of the building had deteriorated considerably. Leaking roofs, burst pipes and a lack of heating caused regular disruptions to school life. After many years relief was to come through the Government's BSF (Building Schools for the Future) funding. Mike Chapman had been appointed Head Teacher in 2006 and led the school into this process. Initial stages involved consultation with staff, students and local residents. Eventually a plan was agreed which would involve demolishing the extensions dating from the 60s and the creation of new buildings in their place. The Grade II listed building of 1933 was to be refurbished in what amounted to building a 21st Century school inside the fabric of a 1933 building. The cost of the project was around £27 million. Taylor Woodrow (now Vinci Construction UK) was awarded the contract.

Both the original and the 1960s extension were in poor condition when this photograph was taken in 2008

The poor condition of the 1960s building by 2008.

Work started in 2008 and lasted three years. Temporary classrooms were installed on the playing fields to cope with classes moved from the old school as refurbishment started. In 2010 the new building was completed to house the Library, Creative Arts Faculty, Sixth Form, Dining Rooms and other facilities. By Easter 2011 the refurbishment of the original building was complete, and a few weeks later the Sports facilities were completed leaving only the external landscaping to be completed in the summer of 2011.

Entrance Hall.

Front entrance.

Main Hall.

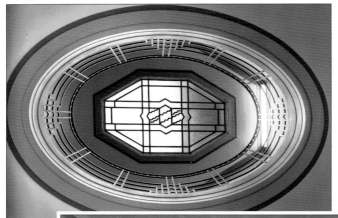

Main Dining Hall.

Dance Studio.

Old Library.

Small Dining Hall.

New Library.

In 2008 High Storrs radically changed the pastoral system from one based on year groups to an innovative one based on houses.

"High Storrs School has a long history of pupils being organised into houses for sporting purposes. In the 1940s these were named after the peoples of Early Middle Ages (Franks, Jutes, Saxons and Normans) and more recently after the teachers who led them; Smith and Stephenson will be familiar to ex-pupils.

In the current system each House of 300 students is comprised of 10 vertically grouped forms (each form consists of approximately six students from each year group.) There are four Houses each one led by a Head of House and a Deputy Head of House. Every member of teaching and support staff is also allocated to a House.

The Houses were named following a competition in which students submitted entries of names linked to a Sheffield theme. Suggestions included twinned towns, famous people from the city, rivers and the eventual winners, after a pupil and staff vote, Sheffield Theatres. This theme recognises and celebrates the school's strength and interest in performing and creative arts and was an extremely popular choice. And so were born:

Crucible House (red)
Lyceum House (yellow)
Merlin House (blue)
Montgomery House (green)

House events including Celebration of Success evenings, Sports Day, inter-house sports competitions and fundraising days are becoming part of a new High Storrs tradition".   Lynne Raven, Assistant Headteacher (Inclusion)

Crucible House.

Lyceum House.

Merlin House.

Montgomery House.

An element of the BSF project was the creation of public art. In April 2011 "The Journey" by Charlie Whinney was unveiled.

This is a 40 metre long steel and wood sculpture that appears to thread its way through the walls and ceiling of the new school building. The brief was to create something that would embody something of the 'essence' of the school, which fosters the creative and academic needs of the individual students in a unique and very positive way.

The design was the result of three workshops and 'public vote' carried out in the school, and collaboration and consultation between the artist, the school and Sheffield City Council.

VINCI Construction UK are delighted to be sponsoring the High Storrs School Commemorative Book and hope you find reading about the redevelopment works carried out to the school as interesting as we did in undertaking this prestigious development to improve the school facilities for the children of our future.

As lead partner in Sheffield's Building Schools for the Future programme, VINCI Construction UK were delighted to be awarded the contract to design and build a new teaching/administration block and a sports hall and refurbish the original 1933 Grade II listed buildings which houses most of the classrooms.

The original Main Hall remained the centre of the school, and a new ICT (Information Communication Technology) system was installed throughout.

The school remained operational throughout the construction works, so due consideration on issues such as noise, dust and deliveries was essential.

VINCI built high quality temporary classrooms, a temporary kitchen and areas for our temporary access roads, car parks, construction offices, and welfare facilities at the top end of the playing fields. We demolished all the 1960s buildings at the north end of the original school and erected hoardings and fencing to segregate the first construction areas from pupil areas.

The project was extremely hi-tech with advanced techniques, and we involved our VINCI Technology Centre to ensure we used the most advanced facilities in terms of meeting future needs and flexibility for high quality performing arts. An example is the use of Weinberger clay block work, which improved building acoustics, allowed us to reduce wall thickness, drastically cut secondary steelwork and speeded up construction.

The works were conducted in seven phases; two for the separate new builds, four for the refurbishment of the area between the new buildings which included restoration of the Grade II listed buildings, and the final phase for the reinstatement of the playing fields once temporary buildings had been removed.

A considerable amount of programme time was lost over the course of the project, largely due to bad weather (three weeks lost in the winter of 2009 and two weeks in 2010). While sympathetic, the client still required completion by the start of the 2011 academic year, and we achieved this by creating more overlap in the programme through regular re-scheduling.

Community Engagement

We held site visits for students to understand bore holes as part of their study of geology.

As High Storrs is a specialist Performing Arts school, we encouraged the students to work on a film of the construction works which involved regular site access for small parties to film and to interview team members on various aspects of the project, such as sustainability. This continued until the end of the scheme in September 2011.

We allowed the school to use our site car park to host a car boot sale, and used our removers to transfer redundant Design and Technology workbenches to a nearby charity free of charge instead of allowing them to be scrapped.

We feel very privileged to have delivered the transformation of High Storrs School and delighted to have provided absolute up to date facilities for the use of staff, pupils and the wider community.

Keith Shivers
Regional Director
VINCI Construction UK Limited

HEADTEACHERS OF THE CENTRAL AND HIGH STORRS SCHOOLS

CENTRAL HIGHER SCHOOL - CO-EDUCATIONAL
1880 – 1882 Mr Alexander F McBean, LLD

CENTRAL SCHOOL - CO-EDUCATIONAL
1882 – 1885 Mr Arthur Newell, MA

1885 – 1899 Mr J E Taylor, MA, BSc

1899 – 1923 Mr J W lliffe, MA

1904 RENAMED CENTRAL SECONDARY SCHOOL
1904 Miss F M Couzens, BA, Superintendent in charge of girls

1906 School divided into Boys and Girls Schools

CENTRAL SECONDARY GIRLS SCHOOL	CENTRAL SECONDARY BOYS SCHOOL
1906 – 1925 Miss Florence M Couzens, BA	1906 – 1923 Mr J W Iliffe, MA
1926 – 1935 Miss Emily M Jackson, BA	1923 – 1928 Dr W I Moore, DLit BSc
1935 – 1945 Miss E M Battensby, CBE, MA	1929 – 1946 Mr Luther Smith, MA

1940   SCHOOLS RENAMED HIGH STORRS GRAMMAR SCHOOLS

FOR GIRLS	FOR BOYS
1940 – 1945 Miss E M Battensby, CBE, MA	1940 – 1946 Mr Luther Smith, MA
1945 – 1969 Miss E M Furtado, BA	1946 – 1966 Mr George Mack, MA
1966 – 1988 Mr T B J Mardell BSc	

1969 SCHOOLS MERGED AS COMPREHENSIVE AND NAMED HIGH STORRS SCHOOL
1969 – 1988   Mr T B J Mardell. BSc

1988 – 1998   Dr Cheryle Berry, BSc, MA, DBA

1999 – 2005   Miss Liz Talmadge, BEd(Hons), MA

2006 – 2009   Mr Michael J Chapman. BA(Hons), MA, CertEd

January 2010   Mr lan Gage BEd, MEd

Some Notable Alumni

This is not a comprehensive list but intended to show some examples of the achievements of former pupils.

High Storrs School

Chloe Newsome, actress

David Bowden, Sky reporter

Jessica Ransom, actress

Nick Matthew, current world Number 1 squash player

Tom Ellis, actor

Andrew Hawley, actor

Jane Irving, GMTV presenter

Anna Lauren, actress

Jack Lester, footballer

Kyle Walker, Tottenham Hotspur footballer

High Storrs Grammar School for Girls

Judith Bingham, composer

Janet Brown, Chief Executive since 2007 of the Scottish Qualifications Authority, and Managing Director from 2000 – 7 of Scottish Enterprise

Pauline Cox, Head Teacher Tiffin Girls' School

Stella Greenall, involved in the introduction of student grants in 1962

High Storrs Grammar School for Boys

David Allford CBE, architect

Prof John Anderson, Professor of Dental Prosthetics from 1964 – 82 at the University of Dundee

Joseph Ashton OBE, Labour MP from 1968 – 2001 for Bassetlaw

Prof Eric Bradford, Professor of Dentistry from 1959 – 85 at the University of Bristol

Kenneth Brooksbank DSC, Chief Education Officer of Birmingham from 1968 – 77

Prof Robert Buchanan OBE, Professor of the History of Technology from 1990–5 at the University of Bath

Prof Edward Clegg, Regius Professor of Anatomy from 1976–89 at the University of Aberdeen, and President from 1988–9 of the Anatomical Society of Great Britain and Ireland, and Chairman from 1988–92 of the Society for the Study of Human Biology

Jacob Ecclestone, President from 1979–80 of the National Union of Journalists (NUJ)

Prof Harold Egglestone, Professor of Mathematics from 1958–66 at Bedford College (London)

Prof Timothy Evans, Professor of Intensive Care Medicine since 1996 at Imperial College School of Medicine

Peter Glossop, opera singer

Steve Heighway, footballer

Paul Heiney, journalist, broadcaster, author

Jeff Rawle, actor

Central Secondary School

Professor Thomas E ALLIBONE physicist

Sir Thomas LODGE Consultant Radiologist

Sir Thomas PADMORE Senior Civil Servant

Harry BREARLEY Inventor of stainless steel

Isidore LEWIS (was Lord Mayor of Sheffield)

Percy KIRKMAN (was Lord Mayor of Sheffield)

Bert McGEE Industrialist (was Chairman of Sheffield Wednesday)

Lord DAINTON academic (was Chancellor of Sheffield University)

Sir Frank Fraser Alistair DARLING - ecologist and nature conservationist

Reginald DIXON (Organist Blackpool Tower Ballroom from 1930 to 1970)

Robert DUNBAR (was Head of Treaty Department, Foreign Office)

Percy DUNSHEATH - Inventor of Pluto, pipe line in WW2